The Power of the Word

JOHN B. KEANE

THE POWER OF THE WORD

With Cartoons by Doll

BRANDON

First published in 1989 by
Brandon Book Publishers Ltd
Dingle, Co. Kerry, Ireland

British Library Cataloguing in Publication data
Keane, John B.
The Power of the Word
I. Title
828′.91409

ISBN 0–86322–108–4

Cover design by The Graphiconies, Dublin
Typeset by Irish Typesetting and Publishing Co, Galway
Printed by Richard Clay Ltd, Bungay

Contents

The Power of the Word

"He is the saviour of our country, the greatest Irishman since Saint Patrick."

"But Saint Patrick wasn't an Irishman," I protested.

"Neither was Dev," he whispered triumphantly.

Letters of a Civic Guard

"Thanks be to God we have our health," said Dick Roche from his wheelchair.

Self Portrait

"Playwriters," said Denis Murphy, "only puts down what we says and charges us to hear it."

Sunday Independent interview, January '89

May God preserve us from the awful stigma of so-called respectability.

Fleadh Cheoil na hEireann, *RTE*

We're not Jack or Tom or Mick. We're Paddy.

Hut 42

A minor bore can be of incalculable assistance in deflecting the attentions of a major bore.
Evening Herald

Applying the letter of the law when you're not a legal expert is like handling a Mill's bomb when you're not a bomb-disposal expert.
Letters of a Civic Guard

Writing about sex in Ireland is like writing about poitín in Iran. The anti-sex mullahs will bid for your jugular.
Irish Echo

There he goes, the man what learned me English.
Limerick Leader

He travelled widely and spoke numerous languages, including Gaelic, Australian and New Zealandese.
Limerick Leader

What crime so monstrous have I unwittingly committed

that I should be visited with this revelation by one of my own flesh and blood?

Be anything. Be a spy, an informer, even a pimp or a whoremaster. Dammit and blast it be a hangman but don't be an actor.
The Crazy Wall

There is no real singular for thugs.
Evening Herald

Man's capacity for character assassination is exceeded only by his capacity for never retracting till his lawyers tell him he had better settle out of court.
Limerick Leader

The achievement of a man who over-writes is as valueless as that of a losing horse which reserves its best efforts for when it passes the winning post.
Owl Sandwiches

If you commit the sin of existing you are critics' fodder until you stop existing.
Evening Herald

The first to work overtime were writers.
Evening Herald

Digressions are to my tales what oases are to desert nomads, what incidental levities are to harrassed religious congregations, what the sideline fracas is to the bored onlooker. A story without digressions is like a thoroughfare without side-streets.
Irish Echo

A man may reveal his sins in confession but he will deliver his all in his letters ... He is dependent for discretion on you and you alone. Often you will convey expressions of the love that blossoms pure in the hearts of men. No trust could be more sacred. Transport these and all other commissions with tenderness and care. I would forfeit my life rather than submit one of my letters to anyone but its rightful owner.
Letters of a Country Postman

He was the literary editor of a toilet accessories magazine.
Evening Herald

False teeth, false eyelashes, false hair, but a heart that is true.
Evening Herald

A play about sex in Ireland is always ahead of its time.
Irish Times interview, November '88

There was a body to her chuckle like boiling tar.
Limerick Leader

I speak four languages fluently. I have a fair knowledge of seven others but in the entire eleven there is no word or group of words which would adequately describe the demon in your midst.
Moll

Her story would bring tears from a hard-boiled egg.
Evening Herald

The river isn't her master for non-stop chatter.
The Bodhrán Makers

He was that kind of critic who loathed sustained applause at the final curtain. His conclusion was that if everybody clapped it had to be common. He would have liked total lack of recognition for the work so that he alone might be credited with the discovery of a new talent.
Comment on a critic

One can haw-haw, hee-haw and hum-haw but a haw without a hum, a hee or another haw cannot be said to compound a meaningful utterance.
Is the Holy Ghost Really a Kerryman?

Sometimes I remind myself of an undeveloped character in one of my own plays.
"Late Late Show," RTE

Pupil "I'm late, sir. My mother's watch: it stopped."

Teacher "You are the misbegotten metamorphosis of a miscalculating microchronometer."
After-dinner speech, Killarney '88

He is a true local. Everything local is anathema to him.
On a Cork city critic

He thought *felo de se* was a chap from Ballybunion.
Limerick Leader

If the gentle reader is truly interested in seeking the source of humming which is musically expressive and yet linguistically effective he should ask one of his relatives for the loan of a substantial sum of money.
Is the Holy Ghost Really a Kerryman?

Poetry is bad enough without it being long.
Evening Herald

I think that poets should cease practising at forty and go

on to plays and novels the way racehorses go on to hurdles and chases before retiring in the end to the pastures of reminiscence.
Evening Herald

The Milky Way has always been a great constellation to me.
Evening Herald

The writer's greatest asset is his indignation.
Radio Talk, RTE

"Iss werry lak chicken," an elderly man confided.
"Nein, nein," says his companion, "is better to chicken. Dis owl sandwich has a real flavour, lak owl."
Owl Sandwiches

"Asses of all kinds," said he. "Splitholes, cutjacks and fullballs."
Evening Herald

Sotto Voce as they say in France.
Letters of a Successful TD

When asked a question she would first scratch some part of her anatomy as if she was consulting a reference book.
The Kerryman

Perplexity is a dying trout on the barb of an angler's fly.
Evening Herald

This fish, like life, is just a cod no matter what the sauce suggests.
Evening Herald

There's no fear you'll catch me manducating with you or anyone else for I was brought up a decent Catholic girl.
Unlawful Sex

There isn't a belly in the hospitals of Ireland, Maggie, would throw up a gallstone half as hard as you.
Big Maggie, Abbey Theatre, '88

There's many a regal gander no more than skin and bones in his pelt.
Limerick Leader

He is a man of ideology, psychology, archaeology and bollixology and a great man too to fix a crack on a ceiling.
Letters of a Matchmaker

As faith without good works is dead so also a corner without a boy is dead.
Unusual Irish Careers

For instance, if your name is John Joseph Soap you might have printed on your card John Joseph Soap N.C. N.C. simply stands for nice chap. Every human being

can be a nice chap and I feel he should be represented as such.
Unusual Irish Careers

He had hair on his ears, hair in his nose, hair on his chest, but none on his head.
Evening Herald

He had a face that begged a kick on the behind.
Evening Herald

To be a corner boy one must be fit for nothing else. It is a career into which men are born, not thrust. A corner boy can, in his own time, become an institution.
Unusual Irish Careers

He had the furtive look of a man who has burst the back seam of his trousers.
Evening Herald

His waistcoat I remember – tobacco-perfumed parallelogram of pennied pockets.
"My Father," *The Street and Other Poems*

Father and son but brothers likewise since the pair of them are sons of the devil.
Sive

How is it they always overlook Anon. when they're giving out doctorates and literary awards!
Evening Herald

There wasn't as much lean on the meat as you'd draw with a stroke of a red biro.
The Kingdom

I have long felt that your strong and silent type is often

an unfortunate chap endeavouring to digest a lifetime of witty rejoinders.
Evening Herald

You don't write Odysseys and Iliads without help from your father. I can see old Homer senior patting the young fellow on the back and boasting about him to his neighbours. "That's my son. That's the boy that writes the epics."
The Crazy Wall

"I had a greyhound during the Economic War," Davy Gunn said, "that polished off a calf a day. He grew to the size of a wolfhound. In the end we could not keep him in meat so we gave him to a circus."

"What was the name of the circus?" the Gortnaminch man asked.

"I forget," Gunn replied wearily. "All I know is that they painted him with black stripes and passed him off as a tiger."

"I remember him," said the Gortnaminch man. "Had he a cut over his eye?"

"I don't know," said Gunn, "but if you don't stop asking questions you'll have a cut over your arse."

This chastened the Gortnaminch man and he asked no more questions.

"A house without a dog," said Davy Gunn, "is like a hearth without a fire."

"Too true," said the Gortnaminch man as he made for the door. "And a house without a liar is like a hearse without a coffin."

Owl Sandwiches

There's nothing as contageous as silence in the presence
of injustice.

Radio Talk, RTE

Free-Range Love

"I'd marry you all right," said she, "but I couldn't leave down my regular clients."
Letters of a Love-Hungry Farmer

When I wore civvies women tended to ignore me but when I went out into the world a fully-fledged, fully uniformed postman I found myself in a new and deadly game.
Letters of a Country Postman

Many a worshipful devotee will tell you that of all the world's vistas the female posterior is the most surpassing. Even the most chaste will not deny that in its unclad glory it is the most intoxicating of all prospects.
Letters to the Brain

Icebergs melt, John, when the warm air circulates about them. Basically there are three kinds of women – cold, warm and hot. Your warm woman is best but there aren't enough warm women to go around so we are left with the cold and the hot. The hot is all appetite and

consumes too much too soon. Therefore we must look to the cold.
The Chastitute

There are all too many Irish women like sportscars, with speeds of one hundred and fifty but moving at only forty-five.
"Late Late Show," RTE

She was the oldest of seven sisters and neighbours who knew them will give evidence that not one of them drew on a pair of knickers till the day they went into service.
Letters of a Civic Guard

She delicately stroked her coif
And thighs as well-defined as if
The garments glued to bulbous flesh
Were far away as Marrakesh
While fatted folk of selfsame sex
She scoffed at and for sure did vex

And showed no trace of shame or fear
It was her time, her place, her year.

[To a girl of eighteen in a cocktail lounge which is filled with old women.]
The Street and Other Poems

She had long legs which transmitted bustle, life and activity to the bouncing buttocks overhead.
Irish Short Stories

Even if I were to give myself to a man I would reserve a part of me which I believe is not mine to give.
Evening Herald

He had the money and he had the appearance and when you have those you get the opportunities.
Big Maggie

I knew honest men and sober men, upright men, holy men and sane men and every one of them was betrayed

sooner or later by a rogue of a dickie, if you'll forgive the expression, ma'm.
Big Maggie

He was born with a pretty face but fortunately for him his nose was broken when he was fourteen.
Evening Herald

"He was a chap of the neuter gender," said Dan, "who lost his contraption when a chairoplane gave under him."
Man of the Triple Name

I have only one life and the Catechism don't say anything about courting or coupling in the hereafter.
Letters of a Matchmaker

When she returned from that rapturous clime where some bewitching form of inducement had lured her,

she could not credit the fact that she was lying on her back and that a strange man had just been astride her.
The Bodhrán Makers

Her posterior stands fast: pinched and patted a thousand times but never surrendered.
Radio Talk, RTE

The cure for homesickness is the opposite sex.
Evening Herald

No more naked gallops for me. Let horses and asses do that. No one minds them.
Values

The thirties was the time of the shut mouth and the closed eye and the hardened heart. There were two big, black clouds covering the pleasant face of the country. One of them was the Church and the other was the State. They made prisoners of our minds and bodies

and 'twas that bleak for a while we were afraid to take note of the beating of our own hearts.
Letters of a Matchmaker

"Listen," said Dan. "If you saw two asses coupling would you question the age of the stallion or would you deny him his share of the natural joys of the world, or if you saw a pair of crows threading would you ask the cock for a birth certificate? You would not, but you'd condemn a Christian."
Man of the Triple Name

"Sex is a fine thing," said Dan, "so long as it don't go to the head."
Man of the Triple Name

"You guys pussy-hunting?" she said.
"Naw," said my friend. "We ain't huntin' for nothin'."
Owl Sandwiches

Given the unlikely options of attending a funeral or a

sex orgy the dyed-in-the-wool Celt will always opt for the funeral.
Limerick Leader

He's the greatest unhung bum in the thirty-two counties with enough of his bastards in this constituency alone to make a football team and a jury.
Letters of a Minister of State

What he fancies is a lady that would be middling fat but firm ... He don't care whether she be grey or black. You may take it from this that he is easy to please for isn't he thirty years on the trail without raising a scent.
Letters of a Matchmaker

Virginity is very like a souvenir: priceless to its proprietor but often worth considerably less in the open market.
Limerick Leader

Maggie (to Byrne the monumental sculptor) "The day you wrong me, Byrne, is the day you'll make me pregnant."

Byrne "All the Byrnes big and small wouldn't do that nor couldn't do that. We would need softer stone than you, Maggie."
Big Maggie

Don Juan never died. He is still languishing feverishly in the breasts of middle-aged men.
Evening Herald

If you have enough money you'll even get broth in a brothel.
Evening Herald

"Could you tell us, like a good guy," said one of the clerics, "where we would find some game around here?"

"Game," said Dan, and he pondered for a moment. "You will go back the way you came," said he, "and you will take the first turning to your right. Then you will take the next turn on your left until you come to a bridge with a hump on its back. After the bridge you will come to a cottage. There's a brace of widows fresh out of England in residence there and, if 'tis game

you're after, you're at the right abode for by all accounts they're game to the tail."
Man of the Triple Name

Basically he suffers from the same ailment that afflicts many of his age group in country places. That is to say, he is without a wife, a mistress or regular copulatory companion. Thus he shares a common bond, a peculiar agrestic and religious legacy that has consigned him and thousands like him to nights of stark loneliness and endless, futile dreams.
Letters of a Love-Hungry Farmer

My relation blamed the Protestants for commanding undue deference and sometimes downright servility through the employment of exaggerated aloofness, and the Catholics for the postponement of the comprehensive and ultimate sexual debauch vital to his mental and physical well-being.
After-dinner speech

Kathy Diggins is knocked up again. They have it down on a baldy traveller for zip fasteners and hooks-and-eyes.
Letters of a Minister of State

Dan stood like a rock against anything and everything which might stifle the right of people to enjoy themselves, the right to kiss and pay court, to love, to marry, to dance and to sing their way out of the dark ages of the Economic War.
Man of the Triple Name

The only place you'll see true brotherly love is in a field of bullocks. They're the most contented of creatures because they have lost their faculties.
Irish Times interview, November '88

It's not natural for a man to sing if he's hurt or wounded so we may take it that he's not right in the head when he's bitten by the love-bug.
Letters of a Matchmaker

The night is for cats and lovers.
Letters of a Civic Guard

Did you weigh up the odds well before you decided to

surrender yourself? What were the odds? This house, this farm and all that go with them for a minute of madness in the back of a motor-car?
Big Maggie

You might say I'm one of the exceptions who proves the rule that only opposing sexes should complement each other.
Letters of a Matchmaker

It will be a black day for Dirrabeg if we penalise a man because he has an industrious penis.
The Bodhrán Makers

I would be for the total demolition genito-urinary wise of all invaders of our female domain ... These foreign gentlemen should be deprived of their procreative faculties and these should be tacked on to telephone poles, electric light poles, roadside trees or ... draped over convenient bushes. Best of all ... they should be spiked outside public places where they would serve as a warning to would-be fornicators and seducers from towns and cities.
Letters of a Love-Hungry Farmer

The city isn't everything but at least it's got store-bought love and that's better than nothing.
Evening Herald

I was seduced by a sixty-year-old deserted wife when I was fifteen. After that auspicious beginning I never looked back.
The Chastitute

According to Father Kimmerby a chastitute is a person without Orders who has never lain with a woman ... he is peculiar to countrysides where the Catholic tradition of lifelong sexual abstemiousness is encouraged and defended by the Catholic Church under whose strictures free-range sex is absolutely taboo.
The Chastitute

Better looking men than I, such as vets, inseminators, insurance agents, seed salesmen and warble-fly inspectors seem to enjoy immunity. You could be a film-star and escape without notice, but pull on a postman's uniform and you're a target for every sex-starved damsel in the district.
Letters of a Country Postman

Is Holy Ireland right and the rest of the world wrong? Why were me and my unfortunate equals chosen above other races to preserve our virginity as if it were a sacred relic? Why us? Why me?
The Chastitute

I suppose you could say that a chastitute is the opposite of a prostitute.
The Kerryman

The garter was the timberline of morality and the plimsole line of security. Can the same be said for tights?
Is the Holy Ghost Really a Kerryman?

Illicit sex is bad for the heart. I do not say so personally but it is now widely believed in continental medical circles that sex without a licence will put paid to the beating of the most consistent ticker. It is also accepted in a limited way by many of the religious who, fair play to them, insisted for starters that it was bad for marriage first and for a number of other things afterwards.
Unlawful Sex

Their wives were too damn good ... they thought it was a sacrilege to fornicate with their own husbands.
Big Maggie

"I say to ye," said Dan, "that if the Ram of God comes this way he'll go home a wether."
Man of the Triple Name

He died accidental when the Turk turned over in her sleep, the whole twenty-two stone of her, and smothered him ... He had little luck with the ladies.
Letters of a Matchmaker

For every one of us conceived in hay-sheds, motor-cars, river banks, alley-ways, meadows, pastures, lakelands and uninhabited islands, there are ninety-nine of us conceived in bed.
Unlawful Sex

Maw, abdomen, stomach, belly! Call it what you will it

won't bring down the swelling. A dainty dame like that wouldn't be setting her cap for our man here if her figure was anyway slack.
The Chastitute

The chief difference between edible gooseberries and human gooseberries is that the edible are completely covered with bristles whereas the human are only partially covered.
Irish Echo

An affair is like an air-filled toy balloon which takes off in all directions when its wind is released. It rasps, snorts, shrieks, squeaks and screeches with passion and ferocity unbridled and then flops on the floor, a parody of its former self.
Letters to the Brain

What a wonderful fellow I would be but for this baggage of reproduction which demoralises my every thought and deed.
Letters to the Brain

"He thinks he's as young as he used to be," said Canavan, "but he couldn't perform now no more than a carcass."
Unlawful Sex

Certainty

This is the place I was told.
See the tall grass lie low.
They rested here and made bold.
Now for a certainty I know.

Take note of this bluebell broken,
The fern mangled and dead.
And look at this for a token,
Here's a hair from her head.
The Street and Other Poems

The Sanctified Life?

When a presbytery gets a new housekeeper it becomes likes a country that gets a change of government, like a regiment that gets a new sergeant-major or like a family that gets a new stepmother. A new housekeeper is like a new moon and a new moon can bring anything from a tidal wave to an earthquake.
Moll

She only made two demands on her Creator: my father's salvation and my virginity.
The Chastitute

I was afraid of only three things in my life: rusty blades, casky porter and parish priests' housekeepers.
The Man from Clare

God is easy-going over there [in England] not like here where He's never done with tormenting people, especially people like us with no substance to speak of.
The Bodhrán Makers

Listening to the two of you Sunday after Sunday blathering about Cathechumens and Israelites not to

mention them eejits of Philistines and Sichemites. Sure there was never a Sichemite or an Amorrhite seen in the two dioceses of Cork and Kerry. There's plenty parasites all right but there's no talk of them.
Moll

Not all confessors are hummers. Some are hawers, he-hawers and ho-hoers while others still are finger fidgeters, nose pullers and lip pursers.
Is the Holy Ghost Really a Kerryman?

He married his landlady, a practising member of the Church of England, and became a prize exhibit of his adopted persuasion. Conversions from the Catholic Faith to its ancient flagellator were rare indeed.
The Bodhrán Makers

Now that progress and enlightenment have deprived the devil of his horns I wonder what proportionate modification they have in mind for God?
Irish Times interview, January '88

Bias is a terrible thing, like the countryman who wouldn't go to confession because he couldn't bear to

tell his sins to a farmer's son.
The Referee

We are agreed that enough people are born into this world for the express purpose of suffering so we have decreed that we shall not be of these.
Letters of a Parish Priest

One of these priests had a pedigree terrier called Rex, a veritable bloodhound for sniffing out courting couples who, when discovered, would run for their lives with the terrier yelping at their heels and the priest loudly enunciating forecasts of eternal damnation.
Man of the Triple Name

"Make chaste, make chaste!" she cried as she rushed towards the confessional.
Evening Herald

The bishop has the cuteness of a pet fox and the long-distance eye of a starving gannet.
Letters of a Parish Priest

"Eugenics," the doctor opened.
"We're not," said a woman in the front row, "we're Catholics."
Limerick Leader

Let those who fear Gods propitiate Gods.
Evening Herald

Jesus Christ had no uniform.
The Field

It's my parish and you're my parishioner. Should I tell you to go forth and fornicate properly and then come back so that I can give you absolution for a worthwhile sin, or should I allow you to decay in your own barren chastitution?
The Chastitute

I've always been a good Catholic and a good mother and you had no right sending me on those immortal books with pictures of naked savages all over them.
Letters of a Successful TD

A WORD
doll

They get [their authority] from a people who have never flowered, an abject race of pseudo-moralists who let their priests do their thinking for them. We are textbook neo-colonialists. We swapped our so-called independence for the tyranny of priest rule.
The Bodhrán Makers

He's a devout hoor all right. He won't be happy till he's crucified.
Evening Herald

My bodily instincts might say one thing but my faith always said another, and my instincts were no match for the faith that was imposed upon me.
Big Maggie, Abbey Theatre, '88

Is it a woman that thought Vatican Two was a television channel and the Holy See under the sandhills in Ballybunion?
Moll

Home is a place where love is generated on a non-stop

basis, the ultimate refuge of anybody who means well, the only place where total happiness can be achieved, if there is such a thing.
Irish Times interview, '89

They'll all want the bull but few the calf.
The Chastitute

Ireland is a nation of Catholics and Protestants, many of them Christians.
Evening Herald

"There are two kinds of priests," he declared. "There are the priests who make themselves and the kind who are made by their mothers."
Letters of a Parish Priest

"Before you become a Catholic," said she, "you've got to go out and catch a cumen."
Evening Herald

Abandon authority and you invite anarchy into your dominions.
Letters of a Parish Priest

I bade the scoundrel beat an ignominious retreat to the native valleys of his own ecclesiastical obscurity.
After-dinner speech, Killarney '88

First and foremost and irrevocably I'm a priest. Whatever little is left after that is your son.
The Buds of Ballybunion

I am no longer the lap-dog of Latin lunacy. I'm a free man.
Letters of a Parish Priest

You must find a pocket for this girl in the mental apparel of your vocation.
Letters of a Parish Priest

"By the twenty breast-nipples of Niall of the Nine Hostages," said he, "but this is the greatest mess since Moses came down from the mountain."
Letters of a Country Postman

The propagation of bingo; the ultimate role of the Catholic Church in Ireland.
Moll

When I was a boy hell was a terrible place but in today's hell a snowball would last a long time.
Irish Times interview, November '88

" 'Tis a long time now," said the Gortnaminch man, "since myself and my father and two other dogs went hunting one Sunday evening. We ruz three hares and killed one. We ruz a badger but he went to earth. What happened in the heel of the evening, didn't the two dogs sit down and start to ullagone. They were like two ladies would be singing in an opera."

"Them dogs is human," my father said.

"How come you make that out, da?" I asked him.

"Them dogs is telling us there's a men's mission closing tonight in Listowel," said he, "and if we start now we'll be in time to renounce the devil."
Owl Sandwiches

Grave Matters

A dead man is no good to anyone except undertakers and propagandists.
Evening Herald

There's enough lies written on the headstones of Ireland without my adding to them.
Big Maggie

Death And I have so many people depending on me, Moon: undertakers, florists, gravediggers. I have others to visit this night. I haven't time to waste on you.
The Buds of Ballybunion

It's the mass-cards they remember when the corpse is rotten in his grave.
Letters of a Successful TD

He responded neither to prayers nor to priestly touch and since they could not countenance his damnation in the presence of outsiders they felt it was in order to construe his final fart as a deathbed conversion.
After-dinner speech, Ballybunion '70

He successfully mingled the safe delights of matrimony with the perilous prurience of infidelity and was ultimately rewarded with a highly favourable mortuary card.
Irish Times interview, November '88

Remember that it is with me, your conscience, you will have to contend at the end of the day, and if I don't give you the nod all your penitential posturings will be to no avail.
Letters to the Brain

I wish God would give us notice to quit so that we would have time to redeem ourselves.
Evening Herald

How proud we would be if we could see previews of our funerals. What a shame the deceased cannot acknowledge the regard of those who loved him not in life but lauded him in death.
The Kingdom

He hung himself from a tree near the house. I swear to

you he would never have hanged himself but he knew my two pigs would pay for his wake and funeral.
Sive

Death Oh me, oh my! Hell, Heaven, Limbo, Purgatory, Fiddler's Green! I'm it, Moon. The rest is sham. I am the only fact. I really exist. Look at the graveyards alone. Every tombstone is testimony to my power. Chin up now. Hat on. Time to go.
The Buds of Ballybunion

He had a hard heart but watery eyes. At funerals he was often mistaken for a tear-leader.
The Gentle Art of Matchmaking

If it were any other day we had bar Christmas I would blind you with the tales of lechery and debauch from people in high places but this is the day Christ was born so I'll temper my words in deference to the infant Jesus and ask you all to pray with me that the sinners of this parish might see the light ere this day runs its course, ere this day takes its toll and maybe dispatches one or

more of these diabolical wretches to everlasting fire, sizzling fire, roaring fire that sears every part, inner and outer, of the human body.
The Bodhrán Makers

I've more time on my hands now with the style of tombstones getting smaller. I often sit on the graveyard wall remembering past generations, contemplating the present one and having a shot at spotting where the future generations are coming from.
Big Maggie

Died in his prime, never drank nor smoked, too concerned about how he'd feel the day after.
Limerick Leader

Most male cadavers were buried in their Sunday best although it was felt that there was no need for shoes. This may have been because transportation of a divine nature was provided at death.
Unusual Irish Careers

The grass won't be green over his grave when he'll be forgot by all, forgot by all except by me.
The Field

Life is the grimmest loan of all, my friend. The interest is too high in the end.
Big Maggie

Where there's a will there's a wake.
Evening Herald

There is many the waster in this vale of tears will have his rump well singed when he crosses over to the other side.
Letters of a Matchmaker

Oh come all good men and true,
A sad tale I'll tell to you
All of a maiden fair who died this day.
Oh they murdered lovely Sive,

She would not be a bride
And they laid her dead, to bury, in the clay.
Sive

There is nothing as common as death. Everybody has a perfect right to it.
The Buds of Ballybunion

If there are to be awards for the living then there ought to be a corpse of the year award.
Limerick Leader

The Joys of Country Life

"You may make hay," said Dan, "while the sun shines and you may stook your turf while the wind blows but there's more to be made at the shady side of a ditch of a wet day working the head."
Man of the Triple Name

You have as much chance of getting a straight answer from a cornered Kerryman as you have of getting a goose-egg out of an Arctic tern. He loves words, however, and that's the only way you'll get him going. Snare him with well-chosen words and craftily-cale-facted phrases and he will respond with sempiternal sentences, sonorous and even supernatural.
"Spirit of Kerry," Ryanair's *Spirit of Europe*

If there is one man that don't look like a pensions' officer, that man is a pensions' officer.
Man of the Triple Name

She spread herself all over the company like a hen preparing to hatch.
Irish Echo

The only instrument she used was a small aluminium

kettle with a spout as slender and shapely as the youngest wand of a willow ... From this spout there emanated a powerful jet of whistling steam strong enough to rise a blister on the most calloused palm or subtle enough to sever the flap from the most hermetically sealed envelope.
Letters of a Country Postman

"If a man isn't apprenticed to hardship when he's young," said Dan, "he'll make no fist of it when he's old."
Man of the Triple Name

May the snails devour his corpse,
May the rains do harm worse,
May the devil sweep the hairy cratur soon.
He's as greedy as a sow,
As a crow behind a plough,
The black man from the mountain Shauneen Rua.
Sive

The truly modern man is he who has never used anything but toilet paper.
Evening Herald

The [whitewasher's] ample belly is strictly for anchorage. His ladder will not be easily shifted. His belly, you might say, is his insurance against disaster. Without it he is prey to every gust and to the assorted mischief-makers of terra firma.
Unusual Irish Careers

One old man said he never had enough of this and another said he never had enough of that but both agreed that neither ever had enough of gravy.
Limerick Leader

There are more species of corner boys than this world dreams of and with the growing urbanisation of the countryside we may wind up with more kinds than we can classify.
Owl Sandwiches

A man stops being a man when there's poverty.
The Bodhrán Makers

A fine bonny boy with limbs as supple as a cat and a grin on his dial like a drake in the rain.
Many Young Men of Twenty

If a man lives at the foot of a mountain he is sure to be influenced by the mountain, or if a man lives by the side of a lake it is sure to occupy his thoughts a good deal of the time. Thus it is with me and corners. I simply cannot ignore my neighbourhood corner.
Owl Sandwiches

I often saw three or four eating out of the one plate and they wouldn't wrong each other a crumb.
Owl Sandwiches

Give me a fair slip and a long course and there's no hare I won't turn.
Man of the Triple Name

There is no such thing as a conventional Kerryman. If you try to analyse him he changes his pace in order to generate confusion.
"Spirit of Kerry," Ryanair's *Spirit of Europe*

I know many who were castrated by drunken perverts.

Maybe they were lucky. Did you ever see a bullock that wasn't content and happy?
Letters of a Successful TD

While such domineering taskmasters were inclined to tolerate crimes like murder, rape and incest with good-natured tolerance, they could not and would not tolerate the sin of idleness around the farm.
Is the Holy Ghost Really a Kerryman?

I see the big, mountainy farmers galloping like stud horses through the shallow water and they dragging their girls after them through the spray.
Sharon's Grave

The bohareen is the last sanctuary of over-worked ponies absent without leave, hare-shy greyhounds and indisposed hedgehogs. It is a true haven for harried souls.
The Gentle Art of Matchmaking

You build a wall you give everybody else a licence to do

the same. You build a wall and you shut out Hanratty's hens but you also shut yourself in.
The Crazy Wall

Daniel M. Didder, Member of the Irish Confraternity of Corn Cutters, will attend these premises on the first Monday of each month. Hours 2 p.m. to 6 p.m. Early booking advisable.
Unusual Irish Careers

These men were totally opposed to five-day weeks, half days and holy days, bank holidays, pattern days and all other days devoted to rest, religion and recreation ... Most of them died prematurely from hurry and worry while those who were opposed to their strictures lived long and happy lives even in this world.
Is the Holy Ghost Really a Kerryman?

Apprehensive as an ass in illicit pastures.
Evening Herald

"It is not enough to have your salmon on the bank,"

said oul' Doran, "and it is not enough to have him in the bag for he's not really yours till you have him drank."
Limerick Leader

Firstly it was regarded as a *fait accompli* that a youth who spent so much time in the classroom was rarely fitted for manual work on a farm. Secondly it was widely accepted that an educated agricultural labourer would be fonder of agitating than working and that the quicker he was shipped off to America or Australia the better for the entire agricultural system of the Stacks Mountains.
Man of the Triple Name

Overcome by passion he bore down upon her. He had only barely completed his lustful act when he was seized by members of her tribe who emasculated him straight away and put him in a cage where they fed him on high-grade nuts and berries till he became as fat as a fool. Then they roasted and consumed him entirely.
Letters of a Love-Hungry Farmer

Would you by any chance be anything to the Minogues of Tooreentubber that used to keep the boar?
Sharon's Grave

If you buy me a pint I'll tell you my life story!
doll

When the Whitewashing Act of 1925 was amended it took full account of female whitewashers for the first time. Regarding female headgear it had this to say: "No part thereof shall fall down over the eyes nor shall the pigmentation and arrangement be such that it might serve to attract onlookers into whitewashing areas."
Unusual Irish Careers

Many young men of twenty said goodbye
All that long day
From break of dawn until the sun was high.
They left the mountain and the glen,
The lassies and the fine young men.
I saw the tears of every girl and boy,
Many young men of twenty said goodbye.
Many Young Men of Twenty

The bohareen is the by-way of the uncommercial traveller.
The Gentle Art of Matchmaking

In the book of records Dandy Keane was credited with landing the largest enamel chamber-pot ever taken by

rod and line from one end of the Feale River to the other.
Unlawful Sex

"My great-grandfather," said a Ballylongford man, "had a greyhound bitch one time, and usen't she stand on her two front paws every time she heard the national anthem."
Owl Sandwiches

"Not by bread alone doth man live," said Callaghan as he sliced the pig's cheek for the wrendance, "but by butter and beer and sausages."
Evening Herald

This is the man who introduced grapefruit to the parish of Lochnanane.
Letters of a Parish Priest

I would much prefer to write about the living lingo of the greater, hard-necked Atlantic warbler known as the Kerryman who quests individually and in flocks for all

forms of diversion and is to be found high and low, winter and summer, whenever there is the remotest prospect of drink, sex or commotion.
"Spirit of Kerry," Ryanair's *Spirit of Europe*

My cows are no fools and they in and out of the Long Acre since they were heifers. They knows the gaps and they knows a bull when they sees one and he knows them.
Letters of a Matchmaker

The Street

A golden mellow peace forever clings
Along the little street.
There are so very many lasting things
Beyond the wall of strife
In our beleaguered life.
There are so many lovely songs to sing
Of God and his eternal love that rings
Of simple people and of simple things.
The Street and Other Poems

"If I could personify this area of rural Ireland," Father Kimmerley told his bishop, "I would see it as an

unshaven lout, 55 years old, wearing a long black coat and a cap. He would be standing at the door of a public house with porter stains on his mouth and a blood-stained parcel of boiling beef under his oxter. He would be futilely waving after the bus to Tubberganban. In short, he has missed the bus of life and now he must straggle home on his own."
Letters of a Love-Hungry Farmer

Autumn's End

With upturned bellies lying cold,
In habits black and striped with gold
Behind large windows of glass plate
Dead, swollen wasps accumulate,
Fat frogs harrumph and blurp in peace
On harvest bellies white as fleece.
And in the wells the water's free
From beetle, bug and buzzing bee.
Soft salmon redden in the pools
And lazy squirrels shout "Down tools!"
Moist, green leaves rest in rotting rust,
Hot donkeys roll no more in dust.
The Street and Other Poems

Primroses set in cosy cushions of curdled green.
Unlawful Sex

Taken in good measure Christmas is the greatest of all known antidotes for bitterness.
Evening Herald

The cuckoo says it all in two syllables.
Evening Herald

Sleet: that which is neither rain nor snow nor good round hailstone.
Evening Herald

First came a single pearl which tapped me gently on the forehead before melting into a celestial tear ... Here was an accredited ambassador from the court of winter.
Owl Sandwiches

No bird of the air has ever spoken so economically and harmoniously of greenery's advent than the cuckoo.
Owl Sandwiches

The elements are the mentors of Kerrymen. They can

patter like rain, roar like thunder, foam like the sea, sting like the frost, sigh like the wind, and on top of all that you'll never catch them boasting.
"Spirit of Kerry," Ryanair's *Spirit of Europe*

There are only two real kingdoms: the Kingdom of God and the Kingdom of Kerry.
The Kerryman

The Holy Estate?

The double bed is the hatchery of every family plot, the blueprint for designing the features of every offspring and a good place to hide under if you're a man who shuns violence.
Owl Sandwiches

The seeds of one argument should not be saved to grow another.
Man of the Triple Name

A marriage without a row is like an apple pie without cloves.
Owl Sandwiches

A marriage without a row is like a winter without thunder.
Evening Herald

It would be a great boost for the children to see their mother a postman.
Letters of a Minister of State

She was indispensable till disposed of.
Evening Herald

"Most of them dames do pretty well," my friend was saying. "They're dead beat at eighteen, but they got the looks left and some have money so maybe they con some guy and live happy ever after which is maybe six or seven months."
Owl Sandwiches

He struck Dan, however, in the absence of evidence to the contrary, as a suanach, that is to say a man not in possession of the equipment to put the human seal on marriage.
Man of the Triple Name

I never dreamed I would rear a son like you. If I knew in time I'd have taken my breast away from you and let you wither.
The Crazy Wall

Gay Byrne "And how many children have you?"

John B. "Only four but I'm making negotiations through the proper channels for the fifth."
"Late Late Show," RTE '68

Your father! A half-starved bockock of a beggar with the Spanish blood galloping through his veins like litters of hungry greyhounds.
Sive

The absence of teeth or, worse still, the presence of black teeth, militated against the chance of middle-aged hopefuls.
Man of the Triple Name

By pure luck I came across as fine a mare as ever whinnied a stallion. She is a woman what have a fine form-sheet. Her name is Fionnuala Crust and after untackling herself from a pair of fine husbands she is getting anxious for the tackling again.
Letters of a Matchmaker

As I sat I recalled that my own wife's eyes are celestial

blue with hints and tints of sapphire and aquamarine. Of course, I wrote a poem once to my wife's eyes in our distant days of courtship. That's the one great advantage in being a bit of a poet. You'll always notice the colour of a woman's eyes. The poet has mighty powers of observation.
Owl Sandwiches

My turn is gone. I lost my place in the line rearing another woman's family.
The Year of the Hiker

And will you love her when she's trying to rear three or four children in a poke of a flat! When she starts to get fat and irritable and has no time to dress up or do her hair! When her teeth start getting bad, when her belly is swollen and her nose starts to run!
Big Maggie

How many times in the grey of the morning did he tumble into your bed reeking with the perfume of holiday girls?
The Buds of Ballybunion

I write poetry for spite!
doll

I would be prepared to see a danger sign erected where there is a long and serious history of in-law incontinence. A simple sign might be the most effective, like, IN-LAW TROUBLE HERE or CAUTION! DANGEROUS IN-LAWS AHEAD.
Owl Sandwiches

He'll make for you the first night like a cow making for aftergrass.
Letters of a Matchmaker

It was agreed that the wife would fare forth on her own to the Pattern of Ballybunion, there to make herself available to a young, vigorous and lusty rustic by no means for the pleasure of the ravishment involved but solely to return home with better prospects of producing progeny.
Man of the Triple Name

The double bed is the last refuge of the fractured marriage.
Unlawful Sex

Marriage is a game which requires only two contestants and there is no need for an umpire or referee. Once the whistle is blown there can be no outside interference, no stopping of play until one of the principals is called off the pitch by his or her maker. That is the final whistle for the partner in question but not for the one left on the field of play. One may start a new game with a new partner if one so desires.
The Gentle Art of Matchmaking

"My wife, Master, was a beauty. I often wished she was eighty years of age so's I wouldn't be jealous of her."
The Crazy Wall

Call every stranger you meet sir and look as foolish as ye can and praise be to the holy mother of God ye'll be a credit to ye're father and mother.
Many Young Men of Twenty

Never give your heart to the man with the swanky talk

because that's the very same man that will give you the crack of a fist if you don't have something in the pan for him when the pubs close at night.
Man of the Triple Name

Please advise as to weight, age, colour of eyes and hair. If widow number of offspring with ages and sex. If deprived of natural faculties, please state ... If short a leg or hand or two, please state.
Letters of a Matchmaker

The reason that he didn't marry up to now was that no one would have him, not even the Hag Hanafin and she gone seventy-nine this Shrove with a whisker around her mouth like furze round a gap and the bare pinch of hair on her poll like the plume of a heron.
Letters of a Matchmaker

I concede there have been successful marriages without resorting to rows but these cannot have been very exciting to begin with.
Owl Sandwiches

"Blasht me," said Dan, "but there was fierce demand for white skin on women and little or no demand for yellow or brown skin and what matter but one was no better than the other inside in the bed or out of it."
Man of the Triple Name

The visitors explained that they were brothers from the banks of Brick River ... It appeared that their aged mother and father had died the previous winter within weeks of each other and that the small farm on which the four had managed to survive until then had been willed to the two.

It was a rushy holding which was always tested to the utmost, year after year, to sustain the eight milch cows which cropped it. The pair had fought a long, arduous battle against rush and water and had somehow managed to keep their heads above the latter. Of money they had but little. ...

"You see," said the older, "it isn't two women we want at all. One will do the two of us grand." ...

"You see, sir," said the younger brother uncouthly, "whilst we might barely manage to feed and dress one there is no way we could support two."

The older brother took up where the younger had left off.

"We are aisy," said he with a grin, "which of us goes to the railings [altar] with her once as the two of us has the same claim on her after."
Man of the Triple Name

You say you wouldn't be noticed in a crowd. There's no crowds in marriage beds, only pairs.
Letters of a Matchmaker

Did he ever give you a little rub behind the ear or run his fingers through your hair and tell you he would swim the Shannon for you? Did he ever sing the love-songs for you in the far-out part of the night when ye do be alone? He would sooner to stick his snout in a plate of mate and cabbage and to rub the back of a fattening pig than whisper a bit of his fondness for you. Do he run to you when he come in from the bog and give you a big smohawnach of a kiss? Can you say that he ever brought you the token of a brooch or a bit of finery? Naw, more likely a few pence worth of musty sweets if the drink made him foolish of a fair day.
Sive

The Raging Thirst

You might kick a Keane on the shin without fear of physical retaliation. You may even stand on his corns or obscure his view at a football game but there is one thing that you must never do and that is spill his drink. The Keanes are pernickety in this respect.
Owl Sandwiches

"Express" reporter "Is it true you don't serve tramps in your pub?"
John B. "Nonsense. I served one of your reporters this morning."
Daily Express

You think this moon that waxed and waned through the crucifixion of Christ, that shone serene on Thermopylae, on Napoleon's retreat, on Hitler's obscenities is going to hearken to a drunken cockerel like you?
Limerick Leader

The Doc Enright had the right cure for the 'flu. First provide yourself with a bottle of Irish whiskey. Go to bed and hang your hat on the bedpost. Keep drinking the whiskey till you see two hats. Time to get up then.
After-dinner speech

I will name but a few of the many staggers which have evolved over the years. We have aided staggers, jaded staggers, group staggers, accidental staggers and staggered staggers. These are only staggers of a kind and, to fulfil a comprehensive stagger, the staggerer must move unaided from one area to another without damage to himself or to others and, in that comprehensive stagger, must complete the entire range of staggers great and small ...

I should proceed no further unless I state here that the backwards stagger is the most precarious of all gymnastic movements. A fall can be fatal and often has been. Only genuine drunkards manage to survive such disasters. There is no psychological explanation for this. It is a fact of life.
Owl Sandwiches

Beggars can't be boozers.
Evening Herald

Lime, which is the basic ingredient of all whitewashes, is a great thirst inducer. Dizziness which comes from having to scale heights also induces thirst as does the business of mixing whitewash. The sloshy sounds arising from this activity are noted for the way in which they induce thirst.
Unusual Irish Careers

A drunken pauper, if his virtues are properly over-extolled and his ego pumped with the wind of undeserved praise, can often be prevailed upon to buy a drink for the eulogist.
Unusual Irish Careers

Before setting out on the skite I made out a substantial cheque to that lovable old rascal known as self.
Evening Herald

There's nothing more difficult than trying to remove a drunken man from a premises where he has had no drink.
Radio Talk, RTE

I remember the time Mickey Moocher's son Patten went amok after flooring two bottles of home-made whiskey in Kettleton's lounge. He crashed into nine different cars, did seven thousand pounds worth of damage, knocked down two people, broke the two legs in one of them and smashed to smithereens the hip of another. Already he had been convicted twice of drunken driving not to mention several convictions for assault and

battery. He had nothing in his favour except the one mitigating circumstance that he always voted for me.
Letters of a Minister of State

A man told me when I was a boy that you could view Ballybunion from several counties if you had enough drink taken.
The Kerryman

Near the village of Ballyduff between Ballybunion and Tralee there is a lovely strand called Kilmore. One fine summer's day several years ago I happened to be strolling along a dune which afforded an excellent view of the Feale River which emptied itself into the sea just below me. All of a sudden a man appeared from the Ballyduff direction. He wore a cap on the side of his head and as he walked he staggered all over the place. It looked as if he must fall into the water at any minute. Miraculously he preserved his balance and as he drew near I noted a glazed look in his eyes.

I could not decide whether he was suffering from some serious physical disability or was just plain drunk. There was simply no way of telling from where I watched. I was joined by a native of the place who happened to be a cousin of mine and a great fellow for country talk with its lovely, native flavour and beautiful nuances. As we took in the progress of the man on the beach that worthy collapsed in a heap without as much as a moan. I was about to rush to the unfortunate man's aid when the cousin laid a restraining hand upon my elbow.

"Fot ails you?" he asked.

"That man seems to have suffered a heart attack," I told him.

"That man," said he in the peerless patois of the place, "is arter the suckund woige to the willage."
Owl Sandwiches

A looking-glass does nothing for me but I do have a face which reacts favourably to a glass with a drink in it.
Irish Echo

Made leering and snarly
By juice of the barley
Curtain speech at Douglas Fairbanks Theater, New York '84

Of course I'm a heavy drinker. Even as a baby I was a nipple tippler.
NBC interview, '83

Here under my very eyes was the one thing I loathed and despised most of all, i.e. a visit from a lout who had done his drinking in other hostelries and then when he could drink no more had the gall to select mine for a sleep.
Owl Sandwiches

I know your father was a great man but he was never as drunk as my father.
The Gentle Art of Matchmaking

When he dropped dead in Killarney all that was found in his pockets was a corkscrew.
Letters of a Parish Priest

What a shame there isn't some kind of degree for drinking porter and backing horses. 'Tis you'd wind up with the high honours.
Letters of a Minister of State

It is indefensible that men who drink for every known

reason and sometimes for no reason at all are not prepared to once toast their guardian angels.
Letters to the Brain

I would follow a box of porter to the gates of hell and beyond if I was dry.
Sive

This was a glittering palace of blinding brightness, its shelves stocked with hundreds of bottles, each glistening with its own individual radiance while scores of gold-labelled Baby Powers dangled attractively from specially designed brackets. Every shelf and every cranny behind the polished pine counter was filled with bottles large and tiny, new and ancient, plain and ornamental. Underneath the counter but concealed from view of the patrons, two wooden half-tierces of stout were on tap, one highly conditioned, the other almost flat, each so primed as to complement the other and to ensure that the creamy white collar remained atop the black stout until the last drop was swallowed ...

Fred Halpin selected a pint glass, examined it carefully for residue and other imperfection and bent to his task. First a squirt from the high barrel and then a brimming flow from the low barrel. Allowed to mingle

on the counter before the customer's eyes. Slowly the suffusion of the brown and white became distinguishable from each other. The creamy head began to form, turning whiter all the time as the brown beneath turned to ebony. There were old men in Dirrabeg and in the other townlands surrounding the town of Trallock who would declare that there was no man born of woman able to fill a pint of stout like Fred Halpin.
The Bodhrán Makers

Public Affairs

Thirty years in Dáil Eireann and never opened his mouth except to pick his teeth.
Many Young Men of Twenty

"Why," one is tempted to ask, "should the bared female posterior strike such fear and foreboding into the minds and hearts of so many corporations and county councils? What is it about the Irish that induces such delirium and hysteria at the prospect of innocent nudity?"
Owl Sandwiches

Oh Cricklewood, oh Cricklewood, you stole my youth away,
For I was young and innocent and you were old and grey.
Self Portrait

All a co-runner wants is your seat whereas the gossip-mongers want your blood.
Letters of a Minister of State

In England all men are equal except an Irishman in a court of law.
Evening Herald

You fought for Ireland's glory
And there's no one can deny,
You filled up English factories
With many an Irish boy.
Many Young Men of Twenty

Emigration is the safety valve of the Irish nation.
Evening Herald

Often when I look down from the rostrum I know that my gaze has rested on at least one man with an innocent face who has an eye for my seat.
Letters of a Minister of State

The law is like a woman's knickers: full of dynamite and elastic.
Letters of a Civic Guard

This is RTE.
doll

Dáil Eireann is the only place in Ireland where the Civil War is still going on.
Many Young Men of Twenty

He was so left of the left that he left.
Evening Herald

Time to end this war and give new wars a chance.
Evening Herald

"If I gets elected," he called down from the top of Gertie Cronin's kitchen table, "every man in Tourmadeedy will get more than the next."
Letters of a Minister of State

He is suffering from an overdose of racial memory aggravated by religious bigotry.
Letters of an Irish Parish Priest

They both firmly believed that the electorate was made up mainly of pathological liars.
Letters of a Minister of State

The minute you don the uniform of the Civic Guards it's the same as if you pulled a jersey over your head. You're a member of the team of law and order for the rest of your life.
Letters of a Civic Guard

The law is to serve rather than expose the community.
The Man from Clare

If Caligula could make a consul of his horse why should anybody be surprised if a politician makes an ass of himself?
Limerick Leader

He'll be elected all right if he gets the Jewish vote in Lyracrompane.
The Kerryman

As the speech entered its thirtieth minute I applied for and was granted citizenship of the land of nod.
Limerick Leader

"When you're done with the law," said Dan, "'tis aisy count what's left."
Man of the Triple Name

Now if you're born poor, my boys
That is a woeful state,
The judge will sit upon your crime
And this he will relate.
"I find the prisoner guilty
And the law I must lay down,
Let this man be transported
Straight away to Camden Town."
Hut 42

I was the lowest form of medical life: an apothecary's assistant.
Irish Echo

Every chronic drunkard in this part of the world will be

putting a number one in front of Tull MacAdoo or if not somebody else will be doing it for them.
Letters of a Minister of State

All the electorate want is something for nothing and they want it now in case there's no tomorrow.
Letters of a Minister of State

The thing is to forage between honesty and crookedness and do the best you can.
Letters of a Successful TD

We are all criminals in somebody's eyes.
Evening Herald

The most resistent of all materials is to be found in the human skull. It can shut off the brain from incontrovertible truths despite the most consistent bombardment.
Limerick Leader

No group has a monopoly on republicanism. Anyone born in a republic is a republican.
Evening Herald

The majority of those unfortunates who are presently incarcerated could well be said to be innocent when compared with those who never close or only partly close doors.
Owl Sandwiches

"It is the way of the Irish," Bluenose shook his head sadly, "we give away our cream and retain the skimmed."
The Bodhrán Makers

Mixum Gatherum

"What kind of invisible dogs you got?"
"I got all kinds. You got kids?"
"Sure, I got kids."
"He loves kids."
"What's his breed?"
"He ain't got no breed."
"Is he housebroken?"
"Well I'll tell ya, he's been here six weeks and he ain't peed yet."
Owl Sandwiches

I ate nine spuds and meat according.
The Kingdom

A sandwich is two slices of barely-buttered bread concealing the dietary inadequacies of that which lies between them.
Unusual Irish Careers

A man who hasn't eaten humble pie has had a mental diet without roughage.
Evening Herald

If you weigh the character of the detractor against that of his victim you will find that the latter always outweighs the former.
The Kerryman

The back is the prairie of the anatomy.
Limerick Leader

Look for a man whose expression would suggest that wind breaking is the last thought in his head ... under that seemingly innocent exterior is the potential for a thousand outbursts, long, short and medium.
Unlawful Sex

He proceeded to hold forth about a last-minute point he had kicked in his twenty-first year. He had taken account of the prevailing wind, of its caprices and inconsistencies and the disposition of the opposing backs as well as those of his fellow forwards.
"More About Bores," *Divine Word* magazine

In much the same way as a Zulu was obliged to kill a

lion in order to assume warrior status so it was considered manly to draw the occasional clout at a referee.
Limerick Leader

Convent dripping will cure all aches.
The Kingdom

Heifer coursing need not necessarily be confined to farmers. City people, however, who would be frightened of cattle might avail themselves of cats or even dogs which could be pursued over specially laid-out courses which might have obstacles like water-trenches or hurdles.
Unusual Irish Careers

There was what appeared to be one small mutton chop or some such article which outwardly resembled a small mutton chop. It was, if I may say so, the smallest mutton chop I have ever seen ... I can only conclude that it was hacked, gartered and hewn from the posterior of a mountain ram when Holy Saint Patrick was a boy on the mountains of Antrim.
Moll

Nothing so affronts the female eye as that cataclysmic calefaction of the culinary world, the sunken porter cake.
Radio Talk, RTE

Forelock touching is a calling which those of perverted outlook who cannot find other employment might well consider.
Unusual Irish Careers

While a willingness to play the sycophant is necessary and the ability to take abuse an absolute requirement, there can be no hope of establishing oneself [as a forelock toucher] unless the basic, perfectly-camouflaged revulsion for one's benefactors is ever present.
Unusual Irish Careers

There is no freedom so sweet as the freedom of a belly released.
The Buds of Ballybunion

Yanks does have their dinner around the same time as we does have our supper.
Letters of a Matchmaker

It is I who refine and render articulate all the explosive protestations of the anus. I am the ultimate processor of every revelation ... It is I who condition and musicalise these uncouth outbursts till they are often no more than prolonged plaints, inoffensive and sometimes amusing to the surprised listener.
Letters to the Brain

Bores have their own code, the major feature of which is that one bore never intrudes while another is harrassing a victim.
"More About Bores," *Divine Word* magazine

He crossed himself and tapped his egg devoutly in memory of his bald father.
Limerick Leader

Lackeys may not be the life of parties but they do most to sustain what life there is.
Unusual Irish Careers

An indulgent soup-maker is often the thief of thyme.
Evening Herald

If only we could package part of lovely and wonderful occasions and then on a bleak day open the package and savour the fragrance of what we once preserved.
Limerick Leader

A wooden leg is like an adopted child. With all the ups and downs in the world it could be better to you than one of your own in the end.
Letters of a Matchmaker

"Throw that barbaric instrument away from you at once," he called out to Donal.

"It is not a barbaric instrument," Delia Bluenose flung back. "It's a drum made by my man Bluenose and the likes of it was never made before."

"It is barbaric," he thundered, "and as well as that it is the devil's drum."

The devil's drum. The phrase was whispered by Delia Bluenose in awe and terror. It was here that Bluenose intervened for the first time: he stepped into the middle of the kitchen and faced the Canon.

"Listen to me, Father O'Priest," he cried with his fists clenched. "Listen wrendance-wrecker and joy-killer. Just as sure as your Christ and mine is the King of Kings so is the bodhrán the drum of drums!"
The Bodhrán Makers

It is left to the noble bear to represent the upright creatures of the world in the process known as hibernation. The bear who is less intelligent than man, according to man, is capable of shedding half of his body fat by the simple expedient of retiring to a cave and sleeping it off. The only thing a man sleeps off is an overdose of booze.
Owl Sandwiches

And what's this story about a hacksaw? Are you cutting off people's bones already? Mind you don't cut off anything else by mistake!
Letters of a Successful TD

When you meet a fool treat him like a fool, that is to say with respect and courtesy, two benefactions for which fools always long but are seldom accorded.
Irish Echo

Of course an old dog can be taught new tricks. If his mentors are the mounting years he'll even share the hearth with the cat.
Limerick Leader

"The man that buttered this bread," said the bishop, "would grease the road from here to Dublin with a pound of butter."
Letters of a Parish Priest

"Well we're not in Greenwich now," said Callaghan, "so to hell with mean time."
Evening Herald

We Irish have a distinct flourish to us. It's like a tail except that you can't see it but by God it whips us around.
Evening Herald

"There's no harm in us. We praises everyone as we goes along. Don't we Jack? I say, don't we Jack?"
Sharon's Grave

There's a hatchery of sin in this house.
Sive

If I could afford a nervous breakdown I'd give it away to somebody more deserving.
Limerick Leader

The ship of night has yet to discharge its mysterious cargo.
Letters of a Civic Guard

Of all colours grey is the most conciliatory by virtue of the fact that it never obtrudes or dazzles and we have noted inflammatory situations where the timely arrival of a grey-haired man had the effect of imposing peace and tranquility on the warring factions.
Letters to the Brain

The grey on his head shows that he has been there and back. The white filaments stand out like stripes on a sergeant-major.
Letters to the Brain

Those hairs thou hast and their adoption tried
Grapple them to thy poll with hoops of steel.
Owl Sandwiches, after Shakespeare

"Beware the 'ides of March," said the Cockney. "They make the worst bodhráns."
Evening Herald

There came a merciful silence during which the clock was given a chance to air its views.
Irish Echo

The sun will singe the head but the moon will singe the brain.
Evening Herald

Go on. Gallop away like the mountainy jackass you are. Gallop away from the sight and sound of God-fearing people. Gallop away into the wind and the wild air where demons are dwelling and sweeping around the bare, windy roads of the sky.
Sharon's Grave

A creaking step is as good as a dog and it eats very little – just a fragment of wax polish now and then.
Is the Holy Ghost Really a Kerryman?

Bibliography

Plays

Sive Progress House, 1959
Sharon's Grave Progress House, 1960
Many Young Men of Twenty Progress House, 1961
The Highest House on the Mountain Progress House, 1961
The Year of the Hiker Mercier, 1963
The Field Mercier, 1966
The Rain at the End of the Summer Progress House, 1967
Hut 42 Proscenium Press, 1968
The Man from Clare Mercier, 1969
Big Maggie Mercier, 1969
Moll Mercier, 1971
The One-Way Ticket Performance Publishing, 1972
The Change in Mame Fadden Mercier, 1973
Values Mercier, 1973
The Crazy Wall Mercier, 1974
The Chastitute Mercier, 1981

Prose and Poetry

The Street and Other Poems Progress House, 1961
Self Portrait Mercier, 1964
Letters of a Successful TD Mercier, 1967
Letters of an Irish Parish Priest Mercier, 1972
The Gentle Art of Matchmaking Mercier, 1973
Letters of an Irish Publican Mercier, 1974
Letters of a Love-Hungry Farmer Mercier, 1974

Letters of a Matchmaker Mercier, 1975
Is the Holy Ghost Really a Kerryman? Mercier, 1976
Letters of a Civic Guard Mercier, 1976
Irish Short Stories Mercier, 1976
Death Be Not Proud Mercier, 1976
Dan Pheaidí Aindí Mercier, 1977
Letters of a Country Postman Mercier, 1977
Unlawful Sex Mercier, 1978
Letters of a Minister of State Mercier, 1978
Stories from a Kerry Fireside Mercier, 1980
More Irish Short Stories Mercier, 1981
Unusual Irish Careers Mercier, 1982
Man of the Triple Name Brandon, 1984
Owl Sandwiches Brandon, 1985
The Bodhrán Makers Brandon, 1986

BRANDON

John B. Keane: **The Bodhrán Makers**

"This powerful and poignant novel provides John B. Keane with a passport to the highest levels of Irish literature ... an important and valuable book which must be read by all who love Ireland."
The Irish Press
"A rivetting read ... It will hold the reader until the last glowing embers of the turf fire die away."
The Belfast Telegraph
"The book has everything, humour, romance and tragedy. There is an abundance of rich characters. John B. Keane can paint the real-life picture of rural Ireland just as Thomas Hardy captured English rural life. *The Bodhrán Makers* is sheer enjoyment to read and it would make a wonderful film. That man Keane is a genius."
Andersonstown News
"A wonderful, wonderful book."
Gay Byrne, *The Late Late Show*

John B. Keane: **Man of the Triple Name**

"There is a wild animal after descending from the mountains and it is the man of the triple name, Dan Paddy Andy."

With these words and many more Archdeacon Browne denounced the last of the great Irish matchmakers, whose "ballrooms of romance" offered relief from grinding poverty and suffocating religiosity. Dan Paddy Andy's character and times, his wit and escapades, are magnificently described by John B. Keane.
"Hugely enjoyable."
In Dublin
"Anybody who enjoys old-style storytelling at its best should reach for *Man of the Triple Name*."
Irish Post
"This lyrical, most human and highly humorous book."
The Irish Times

D.P. Gee: **Hotel at the Edge of the World**

An Englishman is cast upon the mercies of Irish life in a small fishing town in the wild, wet west. Here he tries to come to terms with his supposed role as manager of an ancient hotel. But, lacking the true British grit of a Basil Fawlty, he soon succumbs to the logic-defying charms of his new home.
"Very enjoyable ... both funny and touching."
The Cork Examiner
"This is a nicely written little story in the finest traditions of Somerville and Ross's Irish RM. It cannot fail to raise a smile with the reader."
The Sunday News

Michael J. Murphy **My Man Jack: Bawdy Tales from Irish Folklore**

Joyful ribaldry has always been a particularly entertaining aspect of country life, and bawdy tales have provided a rich vein of popular tradition. In this book readers will find stories, tales and anecdotes which have stood the test of time.
"You haven't laughed at a bawdy country joke for ages? Well, here is your chance."
The Evening Press
"Here is an earthy collection of tales which will provoke chuckles as well as laughs."
The Irish Independent